C000088088

100 really annoying
things about work

100 REALLY AnNoyIng WORK things about

Series Editor: **Lucy Dear** Written by: **Jane Purcell**

Illustration: GWZ.

Page layout: **River Design Ltd** Cover design: **Linley Clode**

Published by: **LAGOON BOOKS**, PO BOX 311, KT2 5QW, UK.
PO BOX 990676, Boston, MA 02199,USA.

www.thelagoongroup.com

Printed in Hong Kong

ISBN: 1904797415

100
REALLY
AnNoyIng
things about
WORK

1

That Monday morning feeling actually
begins about 1pm on Sunday…

2

You foolishly compare your contractual hours against actual work hours and are filled with murderous rage...

Commuting…

During a meeting, the only way to stay awake is to count how often the words 'game plan', 'productivity' and 'target' are used...

5

Because photocopiers are possessed by Satan. They always know when it's critical for you to get that document copied, and promptly break down (after scrunching up the most important page)…

6

Ringing personnel on a sickie, you adopt the perfect Dame aux Camélias tubercular croak. Five minutes later the phone rings and you answer in your normal voice. It's personnel again...

You wonder if you're getting old or does the I.T. department consist of people who still have their baby teeth?

8

Office strip lighting, which gives everyone the grayish green hue of a drowned corpse...

The realization that however much you moan and grumble about work, you're too terrified to leave...

The colleague who keeps you excruciatingly
up to date with her dismal love life…

11

Your telling someone at the tax office to 'Sod Off', has led to the entire company being audited...

12

The little pillock who gets promoted to Junior Vice Assistant Whatever, and promptly starts strutting around in the manner of a person with a gherkin up his bottom...

13

Because the oft-used phrase 'hectic, fun office' means hellish chaos with endemic culture of blame...

After 40 years of work, the net result is a cheap gold watch, a nervous twitch and ulcers...

15

Discovering the socially inept nerd everyone laughed at in school is now the owner of a multi million-dollar software company...

16

School reunions, which so effectively highlight the gap between your ambitious teens and the graying corporate drone you now are...

17

So many colleagues go to the washroom for a cigarette, that whenever you open the door it sets off the fire alarm...

The humble coffee run has become a complex nightmare of skinny frappuccino latte mocha proportions...

Leave your desk for one minute and your 'in' tray will have quadrupled in size…

20

Overhead projectors, which work fine until 500 global directors enter the room. Then they immediately become demonically possessed...

21

A bright-eyed newcomer tells you all about his dreams and hopes for the future. You think: 'Yeah right, I had hopes and dreams once'. Are you really this cynical and defeated? Well…

22

The serial dieting colleague. There are never any papers in her desk, just a million packets of lite'n'cheesy crisps and low fat crunchy bars...

23

Because for all the blurb about downsizing, most of us are working longer and harder than ever…

Because nobody on their deathbed ever
wished they had spent more time in
the office...

25

You need to be a multi-armed Hindu goddess to cope with all the phones…

26

The hospital phones to say a truck has hit your partner and your automatic response is to yell, 'Not now I'm busy!'...

27

The real purpose of the bathroom is somewhere for people to cry…

28

Meetings are like suburban weddings. You don't want to go but are cross when you don't get an invite.

29

Living in fear that one day you, yes you, will be responsible for accidentally downloading a catastrophic computer virus which wipes out the entire network. Then again...

The phrase 'lunch hour' evokes a bitter laugh…

CRACK!

Those office chairs which are thoughtfully designed to turn you into the Hunchback of Notre Dame's double…

The humiliation of constantly phoning the I.T. help desk to say you've forgotten your own computer password...

Being interrupted by some busybody rattling the leaving gift contribution envelope for someone you can't stand...

Work as a temp and it's presumed that you're Too Thick to Get A Proper Job...

The colleague whose computer is obliterated
by furry toys which all have names...

36

You're told about the 'Exciting new challenges ahead' and know it's corporate-speak for 'your new workload would crush God'...

You wake up with a terrible hangover, and realize that photocopying your bottom and shouting at the boss 'Kiss this you moron', might not have been a dream…

38

Someone asks how your child is, and for a second you wonder who they're talking about…

39 Breaking into Fort Knox couldn't be more complicated than getting a new stapler from the stationery cupboard…

The feng-shui office you were promised turns out to be a cupboard with a desk and a fake pot plant...

42

The air conditioning always fails during a heat wave...

The 'coffee' machine that only ever produces evil smelling vegetable soup...

44

Filing. The only things worth filing are your nails...

Being caught by the boss, browsing a 'My Boss Sucks' web site...

Trying to work while the manager who declared 'Deodorants are for girls' is leaning over you..

47

The colleague whose desk has 'witty' signs like 'You don't have to be mad to work here, but it helps'. Don't you just long to replace them with one big sign that says 'I Have No Friends'…

48

The spotty mailroom boy mentions that he's
sad you're leaving and it's the first you've
heard of it...

49

After three years the voicemail instructions still leave you baffled. To retrieve your messages press what?

50

Paper cuts. They hurt something rotten...

51

Those nice people at the IT department inform you that you've run out of swear words to use as computer passwords...

Your lunch break consists of shoveling down a sandwich, during which time, five people scuttle up saying, 'I know you're eating but could you just...'

Annoying chain emails which urge you to pass on the Ten Karmic Truths of the Universe, or your head will fall off...

When things seem to be going well, you can be certain that something is about to go horribly wrong...

55

Corporate speak such as 'restructuring',
'streamlining' and 'downsizing' all mean the
same thing. You're fired…

56

You calculate that if you'd actually been paid for all that overtime, you could have retired to the Bahamas by now...

57

Having to face the office with your disastrous new haircut…

58

A colleague offers you a lift home, and the next day it's all round the office that you're 'doing it'...

59

Being voted to tell the new girl that her breath should carry a government health warning...

Post-it notes always obliterate your computer screen...

61

Discovering the Christmas party has been canceled due to 'lack of funds', yet the Directors have all mysteriously received massive bonuses...

62

The colleague who starts a feud because 8 months ago you ate the last chocolate biscuit...

You realize that every time your boss opens his mouth, you fantasize about his dying in a horrible stapling accident…

If your childhood ambition was to be an astronaut, how come you've spent 10 years in Old Fartz Insurance?

When the photocopier goes on strike, a green flashing arrow appears. It indicates which bit is jammed. You open it, and another unrelated green arrow starts flashing, suggesting the problem lies elsewhere. Once you've dismantled the entire machine, to no avail, you finally bang the photocopier shut, and give it a massive kick. It starts working immediately...

Receiving a funny but obscene email, and instead of pressing the 'delete' button, you press the 'forward to the entire building including head office' button...

The one time in your entire career you pick up the phone and shout 'What!' instead of 'Hello how can I help you?', it's the Managing Director on the other end…

You stand up at your desk and still can't see over the top of your 'in' tray...

Your life consists of work, or recovering from work...

Everyone in the company receives a copy of
The Challenge of Redundancy as a
Christmas present...

71

That moment of truth when you realize
that work is essentially pointless and you
will die without sailing up the Amazon,
learning the piano or smooching
Russell Crowe...

Nobody notices when you work late, but the few times you've arrived late, your boss purses his lips and points at his watch…

73

The fax machine is so clogged up you seriously consider pouring a packet of All Bran into it...

74

There's always someone who spends their time briskly rushing around the office, looking busy and shouting at people. But you never see them actually doing any work...

75

That jolly, lovable boss you joked with at the interview has turned out to be a chronic psychotic…

77

The company manifesto says there's no hierarchy. Until it comes to making the coffee...

When the boss puts his head on one side, puts on a caring expression and says, 'How can I show how much I appreciate you?' you know you can forget all about that pay rise...

There's always a life or death crisis at 5.29 on Friday afternoon…

The Christmas party gets worse every year...

81

Presentations…

82

Trying to change the water cooler...

The colleague who rudely wakes you up during a meeting to tell you you're drooling...

84

Deadlines. Named because even death is a poor excuse for missing one...

The first day of a desperately needed vacation, you wake with a sore throat and high fever...

86

During your beloved grandmother's funeral, you find yourself tapping your foot and glancing at your watch. 'If I rush I could just make that meeting'...

87

Your daughter announces she knows that her daddy is Father Christmas because she sees both once a year…

The profound misery of audio-typing from a tape which largely consists of 'Eurrghh, er bleurr, erm urm, yours sincerely'…

Those 'fantastic fringe benefits' have turned out to be a personalized pencil sharpener and a chipped coffee mug…

The talentless colleague who sucks up to the boss by whisking round his office like Snow White with a duster...

91

All those smug ex-smokers who loudly boast of the working time they're no longer wasting by nipping out for a cigarette. Instead they waste it by pontificating about how much better they feel...

The printing on headed paper nightmare…

93

Computer screens. No matter where you place them in relation to the light, they emit more glare than a disapproving aunt…

For every one item that you cross off your Urgent list, you add another five...

You can remember your boss's bank details
and the birthdays of all your colleagues, but
keep forgetting your house number…

Infuriating desk accessories like spiky rubber fingers for efficient paper flicking. They are no help to you whatsoever...

Over-zealous cleaners who spray eye-watering chemicals into the phone earpiece. You try having a business discussion with the phone reeking of Country Fresh Alpine (Industrial Strength)...

Holidays. What's the point? You just have to work twice as hard when you get back...

99

The guilt of taking an illicit sick day…

Cafeteria food…